The Politics of 'Possums:

A Primer on World Politics

By Dennis Fargo

Email: dennis.fargo@gmail.com

Edited by Katherine Mercurio Gotthardt
Cover Design by Victor Rook

ISBN-13: 978-1506137902
ISBN-10: 1506137903

For Jen

TABLE OF CONTENTS

"The distinction between politics and strategy diminishes as the point of view is raised."

-Winston Churchill, *The World Crisis*

1. POSSESSION

Life according to the animals: Peace enrobed the landscape. The little central valley lay between two barley-covered hills. The two mounds, one slightly higher than the other, pressed in upon the valley, protecting it from weather and capturing sounds that were born there. A little stream ran through the valley and, being shouldered by the hills, meandered along an s-shaped path in order to make its way between them. To keep the hills at a trickle's distance, the stream had fed its banks so that now, a wooded border concealed it on both sides. Each year the little woods grew stronger, returning some protection to the hills with the forward-marching of saplings and a broadening blanket of green.

Summer air carried the delicious bouquet of honeysuckle, cedar and the intoxicating musk of Mule Deer. Opossum, rabbit and ground-hog foraged together at dawn and in twilight. The arcing flight of hummingbirds drew the eye across the landscape, little needles stitching the sky together. In the fall great chevrons of Canada Geese overflew the valley, their honking from lake-to-lake measured by the *shew-shew* of whispering wings. The valley harbored all of its residents in serenity and quiet. The Assembly* - the loose group of inhabitants that moved in and through it - collaborated only as necessary to survive and according to whim. When threats made it necessary to do so, The Assembly debated primarily by thought in bundles of rebuttals – burbles – as it had done for ages. They called the valley The Tani.

> **The Assembly** – In international politics, analogous to the members of the United Nations General Assembly; or to The Conference of States Parties under a treaty.

The Upper Hill had a crease where the rains had carved an access to the creek. The grass beneath the barley grew thick and lush here and erosion had made a flat place at the bottom where grass was predominant and always juicy. The Assembly gathered on that green cushion at those times when secret plans were needed. Cradled in the soft grass, the Plenary Councils* of many generations had rested and chewed together there. They exchanged thought-streams or spoke in reluctant whispers for emphasis. Their upturned eyes would glow in the darkness with reflected inspiration that always came. Listening, they would know what to do. In this way they had prevailed over fire, famine and even the other terrors for which they had no words and were too horrible to otherwise describe to their young.

> **Plenary Councils** – Meetings of all members of The Assembly. In politics, the formal, periodic meeting of representatives of all member states of an international body. For example, the Organization for the Prohibition of Chemical Weapons, The Hague, Netherlands, meets weekly in Plenary Session.

The Tani had been as it was for greening-times beyond memory. None of The Assembly could recall The Protector as a sapling. Now, not only could his top not be seen from the valley floor, but he was wide enough in his trunk to conceal even the largest of The Girls. The Protector and his siblings gave the valley its safety and by the reach of their collective shadows, also its haven. Rising from the valley floor and towering over the hills, The Protector could see all and would gesture and sigh to them when rough weather threatened. Even in the times of hiding when other trees fell, Protector remained. So, the inspirations of the night* and Protector's strength by day had established the Assembly's confidence. Here they were safe.

> **Inspirations of the night** – The Assembly recognizes a higher power, as do many peoples of the Earth.

When Protector was a sapling, the animals known to The Assembly as Tulegs had made war on this land. The bleached fossil bones of cattle, murdered by Tulegs, lay in a shallow depression of The Tani nearest the road, an unspeakable place avoided by The Assembly. Further upstream the woods carried the ruts of Tuleg wagon-wheels overgrown with underbrush and hid gray metal fragments of unknown purpose in its soil. The stream narrowed at the upper end of the valley, where it gargled across pieces of smooth stone with broken edges. The Assembly had sometimes found these strange stones on the upper stream-banks as well; clearly, they did not come from the ground. Because these were foreign objects to The Assembly, they suspected the presence of Tuleg ancestors: none of them living had ever seen Tulegs there.

In fact, there had been no Tulegs anywhere in The Tani for generations. The woods were populated by The Assembly, and it was their domain. Here they could engage in discourse or battle and multiply at will. The Tani was their land and their home. The heavens had willed it to them*: here, even the sky smiled upon them. The Tani sheltered them and they would protect it.

Heavens had willed it to them – The Assembly believed God had given The Tani to them. It is common for native peoples to believe their land is God-given.

2. ENCROACHMENT

A day in the life of the man: On a Thursday in the heart of the city, with spring in the air, an analyst entered the man's office with his brow elevated in proposition. He had seen an advertisement at a local realtor and wanted to share it with his colleague and supervisor.

"Hey," he said in greeting as he walked into the man's office. "Are you interested in any land?"

Looking up from the paper he had been drafting the man responded, "No…no. What land?"

"There's a lady in Maryland who owns a 150-acre farm here in Northern Virginia," the analyst explained. "She has just sold it to a local real estate developer and I know the guy. The sale has not yet been made public. He told me he's going to divide the property into fifteen ten-acre lots. The two of us could make a first offer on a parcel."

"Hmmm," said the man. "I've always wanted to own a piece of land, but at today's prices?"

"I'm going to go look at it on Saturday," said the analyst. "I'll pick you up if you'd like to come along, even if it's just for the drive in the country."

"OK, I'll make the drive with you," the man agreed after some thought. "But I'm really not in the market."

That weekend the two traveled the country roads together under a hazy sky in the analyst's small-bed Toyota pickup truck. Each carried a paper sketch provided by the realtor, showing the farm and how it would be divided into lots. The simple sketch had few geographic features, save for two streams shown as single lines on the paper. Along each of them was the notation, *R.P.A.* The man didn't understand this symbol but would later learn that it meant the streams were designated a *Resource Protected Area* as part of the Chesapeake Bay watershed. Armed only with the sketches, a camera and their binoculars, the two men ventured 35 miles into the Northern Virginia countryside.

No access road to the farm property had yet been excavated. It was necessary, instead, for the two to approach the farmland via an adjacent street with a golf course on one side and older homes on the other. Then they motored past the last house and, carefully, four-wheeled a short distance into virgin woods. Lastly, they made a right turn and accomplished a final hundred yards of bouncing, off-road travel to reach one corner of the advertised tract.

The first time the man saw the land, it called to him. There before him, the synchronized swimming of breezes performed in a sea of green-gold barley that stretched over a score of little knolls. His camera captured the moment with a date mark to freeze it in time. The breeze made the only sound, but he could almost hear the strains of *America, the Beautiful* – amber waves of grain. They dismounted the truck and moved – no, floated - through it, almost chest-high.

Here and there, the visual palette was punctuated with clumps of bright yellow buttercups, and unexpectedly, occasional daffodils. The two men stopped momentarily and struggled to orient themselves with their sketchy maps.

"Let's see, which way is north?" said the man, as much to himself as to the analyst.

Then it became clear. The hidden streams had announced their presence as two tiger-stripes of tree-growth drawn across the available field of vision and were protruding like long peninsulas from the larger mass of virgin woods far beyond. The very contours of the land invoked comfort and security. But the parcel that interested the man most contained the longer of the two creeks. He moved instinctively towards it.

The map he held showed a proposed rectangle-shaped plot of roughly one-by-three proportions that bracketed the length of this creek within the farm property. The two explorers walked along its nearest tree-line, noting the rich variety of growth. Just their first few minutes of observation revealed Sassafras; White, Northern Red and Pin Oaks; Eastern Red Cedar; American Holly;

Flowering Dogwood; Eastern White and Virginia Pines; Eastern Redbud; Sycamore; Hickory; and Yellow Poplar.

"Now here is a worthy piece of property!" exclaimed the man. "Hoo-whee!" The two hooted their excitement, startling and flushing six Mule Deer from a thicket. The deer then stopped, turned and followed the men along the tree-line as if they had never seen a human.

The men found an access through the thick underbrush and made their way to the creek, then walked, teetering on its stones as the clearest available path of exploration. The little stream gurgled its pleasure at being scrutinized, and the valley shared its history as they moved along. Here grew several champion trees, the largest a giant Yellow Poplar over a hundred feet tall. The man could not enfold half of its girth in his open arms. A section of its bark was under attack by Round-headed Boring Beetles. He could fix that.

A line of 30-foot tall cedar trees stretched outward from the creek heading due north, a natural compass perhaps revealing a previous property boundary. Strands of unsupported and decomposing barbed wire lay along one side of certain sections of the creek, giving evidence not just of farming, but the long-ago grazing of livestock on the tract.

Then they found flat stones reinforcing the north bank of the creek - just the north side. The man stared at them and back a hundred-fifty years to his favorite past time – the Civil War. The man, a military veteran, had military history in mind.

"Could this have been a skirmish line?" the man asked the analyst. Both knew the surrounding countryside had hosted the opposing armies of the War Between the States.

The man recounted to himself: in this part of the county, the Confederates, under Robert E. Lee, included the forces of Major General Thomas S. "Stonewall" Jackson; Lieutenant General A.P. Hill's 3rd Corps with Major General Harry Heth's and Major General Richard H. Anderson's divisions; and Major General Richard S. Ewell's Corps. Their cavalry, under Major General J. E. B. Stuart and his trusted Brigadier General Wade Hampton, along with the partisan forces of Captain John Singleton Mosby, had ranged, camped, and raided throughout this area.

He knew the same land had hosted Federals under Major General George G. Meade, especially his 5th Corps; and Major General Governeur K. Warren's 2nd Corps. Federal cavalry including the 13th Pennsylvania had camped and raided here during most of the war. Not five miles away, Maine and Minnesota had fought North Carolina*, together losing 1900 of their citizens, and, well...

> **Maine and Minnesota fought North Carolina** – The Battle of Bristoe Station, Prince William County, Virginia, October 14, 1863. The land near the Tani had a turbulent history.

The man shook his head as if to clear battle-smoke. Breaking his historical reverie, he moved further along the bank, finding a circular entrance to a burrow large enough to receive a Border Collie walking upright.

"I wonder if this is occupied, " the man pondered aloud. "And if so, by what?"

Then, along with evidence of the past cruelty of man, the land yielded evidence of the present cruelty of nature. He noticed that there were two hills, knolls really, within the plot he was exploring – one hill on each side of the creek. Within the tree-growth on the side of the upper hill stood a tortured cedar tree. Its twin trunks, each six inches in diameter, rose in a "V" to a height of seven feet, where they had been bent completely back to the earth, two great archer's bows pointed directly skyward. Not only were these trunks strangled by vines, but the tree's remaining top-growth was held fast, close to the ground, entirely overwhelmed and smothered beneath a sea of Virginia creepers.

Now his excitement began transforming to serious assessment. He moved away from his friend for solitary exploration of the north side of the creek and its wood-line. The trees here were being overpowered by large climbing vines. Many of the trees had trunks that had grown in a spiral, like the legs of old English furniture. Some foliage, entwined in mortal combat with one or two large vines, had been crushed to the ground. Other vines had climbed directly upward into tree-branches and, growing along with their hosts, now extended 25 feet or more from the earth and were the thickness of his forearm. The largest branch of one tree had actually grown into an "S" shape, first up, then downward and up again – a natural sine wave - extending outward from its trunk more than ten feet in its flight from pursuing creepers. Some were not trees, but only suffocating shapes buried beneath kudzu and its kin. They cried out to him for rescue – and he heard them.

Oh yes, he could do something about that, and about the all-choking vines around the dual-trunked cedar tree. He had decided. This would be *his* land, and he would care for it. The place was a haven, to a former sailor like himself, a cove. And the history the land revealed to him gave it special significance. His analyst friend decided not to buy – too much development required. The man saw the challenge, but had the confidence of spirituality. He knew his prayers had been answered many times before. He would pray to Mary* of Nazareth, mother of Jesus – sometimes known in scripture as The Quiet Light - that his purchase could be consummated. His bid for the property was submitted that same week. If successful, he would call it Quiet Light Cove, in Her name.

> **Pray to Mary** – The man also believes in God as a higher power. In international politics, it is not uncommon for antagonists on both sides of an issue to invoke The Almighty in order to justify their actions. For example, the belt-buckles of the German Wehrmacht in World War II were embossed with raised letters, *Gott Mitt Uns*, or God With Us.

But neither The Assembly, nor the man, knew of the other's claim* to the land.

> **The other's claim** – A claim by two or more nations or nation-states to the same territory is the source of much world conflict.

3. GUERILLA LEADERSHIP

Life according to Grundy: It was a good day to dig. The warmth of the air had wakened him where he lay, curled and disheveled, in the dark of the apartment. The holiday had been long and restful. Now, the air stale in his lungs and with his mouth beginning to salivate, he would climb upward toward the morning light, s-t-r-e-t-c-h and exercise unused muscles. And of course, feed. Crunchy thistle was his favorite. For five greenings, he had grown and prospered in this same apartment. The mass of his fur, now bigger and darker than those of his clan-mates, accentuated a fighting weight equal to two of theirs. His square snout and sharpness of eye attested to his full maturity.

His face and fur had been scarred by scores of victorious encounters for contested land, most of those with his own kind. Only the foolish among them would now disregard his penetrating gaze. He had once survived an encounter with a Red

Fox, releasing the jaws that mangled his rear leg by biting off a piece of the fox's ear. He would walk with a limp for the rest of his days, ordering his life among The Assembly with a grumpy charisma. But today was not for walking – he would dig a fresh new room for his apartment instead. The Assembly called him Grundy, and for his wisdom and militancy, he had become their natural leader. Grundy was a Marmot.

Long ago, before his mother had whistled for him to hide and was gone when later he had dared to venture out, she had taught him many things.

"These are my lessons," she had burbled. "First, you must eat when shadows are long."

"Why, Matka?" Grundy burbled back. "So that you may live," she communicated.

"You must remain in sight of your apartment," she added.

"Why, Matka?" Grundy burbled again.

"So that you may live! Now, open your mind for the others!" she scolded.

"You must take refuge when something seems not to be right. You must renew your apartment by expansion in order to confound your enemies. You must stand tall for frequent safety sweeps, and drop flat into the grass when surprised in the open. You must run flat out if threatened. You must defend your apartment surroundings, and especially, must never be intimidated face-to-face."

And she telepathed more. With wrinkled snout, she had emphasized her most important lesson:

"The tall, erect animals who pass through The Tani from time to time are called Tulegs* and are not to be trusted. Although we don't know with certainty, they have long been associated with the mysterious disappearance of some of The Assembly," she burbled.

Grundy learned these lessons well, especially the last. In Grundy's world, suspicion was law, if you wanted to live.

> **Tulegs** – Tall, foreign beings that stood erect; the beings Grundy's mother had warned him about, and who subsequently encroached upon and invaded The Tani; human beings. While his mother probably said, "two legs," Grundy understood the term differently. In politics, slang terms are often applied to an encroaching people, especially on borderlands.

§

The Girls had innocently brought Grundy word of their encounter with strange, tall visitors the previous day:

"There are strange and wonderful happenings on the upper hill," they had burbled. "There are some new but different members of The Assembly, very tall, and we walked with them."

Grundy shot them a quick, stern glance of disbelief.

"They liked us," said the lead doe, deflecting Grundy's displeasure.

Grundy was struck too thoughtless to respond. Of all the potential dangers that had threatened The Tani during his lifetime, this was by far the most sinister, not only because The Tani had been penetrated, but because of The Girls' complacency – they had no sense of their obvious peril. Tulegs in the Tani! Their naiveté made the entire Assembly vulnerable. It was plain that increased education and vigilance by all would be required. He must gather his thoughts. Meantime, he made a mental note:

MUST BURBLE DANGER TO GIRLS!!
ALSO TO ASSEMBLY!

Grundy's annual obligation to make The Call required additional vigilance. Protocol required that he expose his presence during the greening, when the burning in his belly told him it was time, and ramble over great distances to find and visit Suzette, his mate of the previous spring … or … perhaps …

another of her kind. He could not be sure exactly where Suzie had wintered, only the general direction of her last sighting. But Nature did not require him to be overly selective, only consistent. And *there* was the danger.

He much preferred to handle matters of security by himself. But in this case, the others must be involved. All were affected. All must respond. And if he was to remain their leader, he had no choice. He would call for a plenary meeting of The Assembly in a Grand Council.*

> **Grand Council** - The particular name that Grundy gives to his plenary council meeting.

4. SANCTIONS

Life according to the man: The man loved the land more with each visit. Even before he had signed a construction contract, he would visit The Cove just to look at it, to be still and listen. There being no access road, it was necessary to traverse the knolls from the main road in his four-wheel drive vehicle. The direct route to his lot took him down a short, overgrown tractor trail, across three of the adjacent, as yet unsold lots, and through an area of standing water. From that low-point, he could motor up the back of the lower hill that would be part of his land. Reaching its modest summit, he would park in the scrub of its many grasses, out of sight of the road.

There, he would sit on the open tailgate of his truck, drink the air and bottled water, and listen to neighborhood news brought by buzzing insects. Kicking his feet, he would munch his lunch and imagine where best to site his house. He must have paced it off a hundred times, length by width, then finally staked it out for the builder. A hundred times more, he contemplated improvements* he would make to groom and restore the property.

> **Improvements (Sanctions)** – Limitations placed by The Tuleg upon the presence and activities of plant and animal life at The Cove and on the land itself. In politics, sanctions range from fines or restrictions placed upon individuals, to the total maritime blockade of a nation. Usually intended to dissuade an opposing government from some particular action, sanctions sometimes deprive goods and services to the people of the objective nation, thereby increasingly impoverishing and infuriating them. It is easy for the object population of sanctions to perceive them as acts of war.

There were the chuck-holes, for example. He would fill those. *The chucks could not dig here.* The man loved nature and had no desire to harm the wildlife – he just wanted the critters to relocate, off of *his* hill. He would use the earth displaced by digging his basement to that purpose. Then there were the climbing vines: he could easily see that sections of the woods would be denuded within a few years if he did not cut them back. *They could not grow here.* He would make it his quest to save the host trees, carefully unwrapping each branch as necessary, and revel in the increased growth of their subsequent springs. Some vines would need to be torn out at the roots, others, merely cut back – he did not wish to remove entirely the natural wildlife shelter they provided.

And of course, the remaining areas of barley growth, already compromised by Common Vetch, Red Clover, Dandelion, Smooth Crabgrass, and a host of other weeds of all varieties, would become lawn. *The land must be groomed.* For this he had purchased a zero-turn riding lawnmower, using the equity from the sale of his previous home. A Hustler. Twenty-five horsepower. Ten gallons of gas. Sixty-inch swath. The thing would do 13 miles per hour forward; about ten in reverse, heh. When the dealer later delivered it to the property, the man pointed to the young Sumac trees interspersed in the untended barley field – some had trunks an inch in diameter - and asked,

"Will this thing cut through those?"

The dealer replied, "Mister, this mower will cut anything that will fit beneath its blades."

While the county conducted its glacial, six-month, four – turn the page – four, review of his building permits, the man continued his exploration of The Cove. In a shallow depression near the access road on the side of the upper hill he found a strange, whitish outcropping of rocks. But no! Closer examination brought surprise: these were cattle bones! Dried and bleached by time, pieces of vertebrae more than four inches wide were scattered among huge femur, shoulder, and pelvic bones. Cattle had been butchered here. Well, *this revulsion could not remain.* This find so disturbed the man's sense of serenity that, without thinking further, he collected and discarded three alligator bags full of bones, as many as he could see.

At the farthest upstream reaches of his property, he found a few pottery shards on the soft bank of the creek. Could these have been left by the Manahoac or the hunting Mattaponi?* More barbed wire hung with white porcelain insulators – formerly, an electric fence – marked the nearby boundary. *This he would cut away.* Along this north property-line, under a patina of greenish oxidation, he found a solid copper bucket with a wooden handle. It had been smashed perfectly flat. By whom, he wondered, and for what purpose? Homemade breast-shield from the civil war, or just discarded kitchenware?

The Manahoac or the hunting Mattaponi – Two American Indian Tribes native to Virginia. International politics is sometimes exacerbated by the presence and/or movement of indigenous peoples, especially through borderlands. For example, this is one root of the Israeli-Palestinian and Kurdish-Turkish conflicts.

At last came the week when the private access road was cut, winding its way over and around the knolls of the 150-acre farm in sinuous advance … as deliberately … as a foraging … Blacksnake. It cut a 60-foot wide swath through the peninsula of trees, directing the creek through a pair of large culvert pipes, separating the man's property from the lot opposite it across the access road and opening the way for development of the other lots deeper in the tract. The same operation also established the road-berm, turning back the topsoil on both sides of the access road to form swales for drainage.

The grading signaled the man to cut his own driveway. Property development required this challenge be met as a first step. In order to build on the lower hill, at the rear of the lot, his driveway would have to cross the creek. *He would build a bridge.* After careful review of available approaches, he decided on a crossing where the creek was shallowest, as this made the most engineering sense. Hmm – he *did* notice various animal tracks there, too. Deer, obviously. And smaller tracks showing five toes, probably 'coon. Perhaps the shallow area served as one of their watering spots? No matter. He cut the driveway from the access road directly into the valley, between the hills and along the creek to the shallow spot. This path had the least impact on tree-growth, only the presence of a few interfering saplings indicating this route might have been an overgrown tractor trail of yesteryear. *The saplings had to go*, and they were removed.

Unfortunately, the county required the bridge over this trickle of a stream to be built to withstand the 100-year flood. Meeting this requirement entailed digging to a depth of two feet in the creek-bed to pour concrete foundations, accomplished in driving October rains while pumping upstream water around the site. Then, concrete walls were erected five feet high on the foundations, through which passed a pair of 42-inch diameter culvert pipes. The drive arched up and over them and the stream. Lastly, since a gravel surface would only wash away, the man black-topped his driveway.

While the contractor dug the foundation for his house, the man made himself available on site. He occupied himself by cutting the largest of the climbing vines at ground level, beginning with the ones at the tree line nearest the dig. Once the vines were cut, he ripped them out of the tree-tops in a great, one-man tug-of-war. Such satisfaction! Then he *had a split-rail fence installed* on the two long sides of his property so he could better visualize the area he would be maintaining. This, like the driveway, also cut through the north-pointing cedar tree line. A deer trail ran beneath the cedar trees, so he left an opening in the fence at that location, through which deer and other wildlife could pass easily.

To install electric power while respecting the RPA, he rejected the outlandish desecrations proposed by the electric power company: 30-foot-wide rights-of-way to be clear-cut through the RPA. He dug his trench, instead, well clear of the tree line at all points. But this *required the breaking up of rock strata* with a hoe-ram for a distance of 130 linear feet along its path. To deliver voltage reliably at the back end of his ten-acre lot, the man *installed two step-up transformers* along the cable's length, in open field areas.

Installing the water well was easy, but the pipe had to be sunk 440 feet to find and pump sufficient volume. The septic field was another matter. The developer had planned for two such fields on the lot, one on each of its hills. But, when tested, the field closest to the house would not yield a four-bedroom perk. Luckily, the upper hill did, and the field was built there. *Septic effluent was pumped* from the house, down the lower hill, under the bridge, down the driveway and along the roadside tree-line *to the upper hill*. A polyvinylchloride marvel of engineering! To provide furnace fuel, the service provider sunk a propane tank on the side of the house, and the man and his contractors could then dust off their hands and celebrate completion of site development as a job well done.

Now to sit back, watch the tradesmen finish construction of his house and enjoy some of that wonderful wildlife that had attracted him here!

5. TERROR

Life according to The Assembly: One quiet morning, the sky a watercolor wash in grays and blues, a couple of giant, roaring animals* came into The Tani and *ate the earth*! Oh, horror! These animals ran without running and made fire-smoke but did not burn. Great pieces of The Tani disappeared magically, incredibly beneath them, leaving bare earth! The Assembly had never seen their kind and was terrified. Those who could ran or flew for their lives to more distant woodlots, some going miles. Some never returned.

> **Giant, roaring animals** – Bulldozers. In international politics, bulldozers are the frequent tools of those who would establish, demolish or relocate refugee camps.

For those who remained, there began a time of hiding* and great fear during which they endured painful sounds they had never before heard, were choked by more foul smells than could be mentioned and imagined a thousand times their own deaths by crushing, grinding, dismemberment or worse. This was a horrifying period of more than three full moons during which they remained as far back in their apartments as possible or under the densest brush. They ate little, slept fitfully and feared the dawn.

Time of hiding –Usually, the winter hibernation of The Assembly. In this case, refuge from bombardment of the senses. High-decibel sound is used both in prisoner-of-war camps to break down resistance and to discourage or dislodge refugees or migrants from settlements.

When they did venture out, they saw sights they could only have imagined in nightmares. The Tani itself had been transformed! Where there had been shelter, The Tani now opened to the sky for a distance of three tree-lengths. Beneath the opening, the ground had turned black, smooth, and hard. A huge, whitish mound of stone now stood where their favorite water-stop had been, at the flat place where there were no stream-banks and the water was easy to drink. Dismembered trees,* at least that's what they looked like, stood in a row on each side of The Tani. Their grotesquely interlocked branches did not bloom during the next greening.

Dismembered trees – The Tuleg's split-rail fence. Fences are sometimes used as political instruments between nations to restrict travel, trade or the influence of ideology.

And it had not ended. A huge apartment had been dug into the lower hill, and by the size of its opening, was probably built for the great smoking animals. Just the sight of it and the thought that the fire-smokers would remain in The Tani were enough to drive the most timid of The Assembly back into their apartments to contemplate relocation. And new types of animals appeared that preyed even upon The Tulegs. As The Assembly watched in astonishment and disbelief, these animals would pass through The Tani carrying living Tulegs that could be seen squirming in their stomachs!

As time passed, more Tulegs became regular visitors, most often to the lower hill. There, they piled large sticks directly on top of the fire-smoker's apartment.

"This must be a trap set by The Tulegs for the fire-smokers," burbled a fox, always quick to notice digging in the earth. "Perhaps The Tulegs are our friends, after all."

"It cannot be for our benefit," countered Grundy, "because The Tulegs are *not* our friends."

Then the sticks transformed themselves into something with the appearance of a huge beaver den, but not as well made. And Tulegs continued to move into and out of it!

"It must be that The Tulegs have entered a treaty of some sort with the fire-eaters," burbled Priscilla the opossum, expressing her natural concern about bargaining with others for use of an apartment.

Grundy responded, "If this is true, such a formidable coalition would be disastrous to the valley, and will not stand!" He had to disabuse them of wrong-thinking.

It became clear to all that some type of action was needed, and the sooner the better.

6. DIPLOMACY

The Assembly takes action: The cool air presaged autumn groping around for its first day, while a great stirring in the grasses and in the valley foretold the night of the Grand Council. From above, The Protector hushed at them with a soft sigh of mature leaves, one of the most sacred sounds of the valley. Even the stream lay quiet, reflecting a moon in shards. The Assembly slowly collected itself, gliding or scurrying in from above, within and beneath all corners of The Tani. They gathered by ones and twos, moving cautiously and with stealth against their instincts as they dared to congregate.

Grundy sat quietly at a focal point of their sacred space as their numbers grew. Patience was a hallmark of his leadership. He knew his message and the way it would be delivered were equally important. And he knew that tonight's message was of key significance to their collective future – it must be delivered with conviction. He knew, too, that The Assembly was remarkably resilient. Theirs was a culture of optimism. They naturally sought harmony in their environment. They were survivors. He watched with concealed pride as his wood-mates appeared.

Red-Bellied Woodpecker was a skeptic. He remained on a high branch overlooking the gathering and chuckled as they gathered – he had seen these things before.

"Chuk-chuk," he laughed. Then he burbled to anyone who would listen, "There is always some fool willing to disrupt what could otherwise be a productive meeting. Just watch!"

Priscilla 'Possum arrived with an anonymous apartment mate, and the two sat quietly together on the slope. They looked wiry and vagabond, as though they had been awake all night – they had obviously not brushed their hair. But their faces reflected concern, and they seemed attentive.

The Raccoons tumbled in, nervous and clownish. They kept changing their places, as was their way. Grundy knew instinctively that it would be difficult to get and hold their attention. Even as his eyes met theirs, they began scratching themselves, each other and the earth around them. Grundy did not entirely understand their dialogue: when they burbled as they were doing with each other now, it was rapid-fire and sounded to him like, "Abbada-dabbada." He would ask them to enunciate their interventions.

Harry Hawk sat on the fence overlooking the entire slope of the upper hill and kept one wary eye on the Woodpecker. A few Turkey Vultures, infrequent visitors to The Tani, dropped into the tree-tops and folded their great wings, wondering if the group had gathered around carrion. They said nothing, but their naked skulls had the blank stares of cadavers, and they drooled where they sat. *Creepy*, thought Grundy.

The Girls, about a dozen, gathered at the back of the group, some standing, others lying in the grass, but began chewing immediately. And they grumbled:

"What's so special about this? This is just another night in the field," one of them burbled to the group.

"A waste of time," burbled a second.

Still a third communicated, "I'd rather be grazing the clover while it is still moist!"

The Girls typically spoke as one* and in brief monosyllables. In the pending debate, Grundy expected to hear low tones from them, emphatic of their displeasure at being cited as naïve. He would need to focus them on the larger issue.

> **Typically spoke as one** – The Girls would often speak or vote as one entity, through a spokes-doe, in order to increase their influence. This mirrors the pull of a political party or of a group of banded nations in national / international voting, respectively, as opposed to the exercise of individual voting by its members. For example, at the United Nations, the so-called group of Neutral and Non-aligned Nations, or NNA, often votes as a block.

Red Fox, if he bothered to show at all (ah, but there he was, pacing the perimeter and eyeing the smallest of them, distracted by his instincts) could be expected to be cynical and not likely to commit to any plan.

The mice and voles materialized from, well, everywhere. A score of them appeared from the very ground upon which the group gathered. They were all closely related, carrying the same family name – Musmus – and like The Girls, were inclined to vote as a block. This could be unhelpful. Grundy wished to avoid a false consensus. They kept up a continuous, annoying chatter as their numbers grew. He didn't mind their fidgeting, but tonight he needed them to concentrate.

Then entered Suzette! So she *was* still here! She was dark and sleek, with pointed features – he had nicknamed her Seal-Face, but she had not liked it. Seeing her now made his whiskers twitch, causing momentary, involuntary movement of his jaw left and right.

Just as Grundy was about to convene, Aristophelia, their resident Snapping Turtle, entered by step-wise advance, and more than fashionably late. She stopped near the front of the group, dropped to the ground and, seeing there was nothing but Grundy to watch, withdrew into her shell to listen. She could be a strong ally. Her arrival signaled a rough quorum of The Assembly.

Those who had gathered were the most dedicated of the group, Grundy knew: The Inter-Assembly.* Even so, they were not inclined to agreement. But it was their inattention that bothered him most. He needed to make them understand. With a look of determination, he pressed his paw into the soft earth and willed them to a respectful order.

The Inter-Assembly – Representatives of the most prominent and influential inhabitants of The Tani. A parody on the Interagency group that gathers to formulate policy in the United States and other nations, in which representatives of the various departments of government often struggle to reach consensus on a way forward.

Then he began his magnum-burble:

"The nature of the Tuleg's encroachment upon The Tani is unprecedented in our lifetimes," he communicated.

"Not so ba-a-a-ad," burbled one of The Girls in interruption.

Grundy fixed a stern gaze on The Girls, who fell silent. Then he continued:

"The disturbance of peace and quiet in which we raise our young constitutes harassment enough," he noted, "but when it continues for so long, as it has, it becomes an assault on our way of life."

"Yes! Yes!" burbled several mice in stereo unison.

"That *It,* The Tuleg, persists in digging in the earth is heinous to The Assembly, and particularly so to me and my kin, for whom the earth is shelter and home."

"Y-e-a-a-y," burbled the agreeing opossums, as if in English Parliament.

"Even worse, *It* digs destructively and irreparably, a great travesty which cannot be tolerated. *Its* activities therefore must be stopped!"

"Whatever," moaned one of The Girls. "Whoo-hoo, look at you!" chimed an owl. But the energy by which Grundy delivered this last statement caused a couple of raccoons to somersault in their excitement, while jabbering unintelligible concurrence. One collided with an opossum, who pushed back. Birds twittered in the trees. The fox paced, agitated. A skunk raised its tail in excitement, then remembered where it was. Soon, The Assembly resettled itself in the grasses and trees, regaining what little composure it had had.

"However," Grundy paused, "even though Matka's teachings included inevitable incursion and periodic destruction by Tulegs in The Tani, I believe The Tuleg can be reasoned with."

"Matka-shmatka," whispered one of The Girls, heard only by her mates. But they all had known and respected Matka as a matriarch.

"Remember that diplomacy must always be the first option to be pursued," Grundy burbled, "especially by civilized inhabitants." This statement caused a number of The Assembly to raise their heads proudly.

Grundy continued. "And since we have little chance of ejecting The Tuleg outright from The Tani, I believe our plan should be one based upon diplomacy. Ours will be a Coalition of the Righteous.* My plan is to seek to engage The Tuleg in a treaty by which *Its* behaviors can be made tolerable to The Assembly, and perhaps even extinguished altogether over time."

Coalition of the Righteous – Grundy was convinced that his perception of events was the only accurate and rightful one. A similar stance can be taken in international politics, where a declaration of moral primacy is sometimes used as a mandate for subsequent behavior.

To implement this plan, and to do so with the support of The Assembly, Grundy found it necessary to deliver his first-ever Five-Paw Proclamation.* Assuming his most assertive posture and fixing his most serious – some would have said, severe – gaze, he pressed his paw into the earth for emphasis as he unfolded each major point of his plan and silently willed them to understand.

"Our aim," he burbled, "will be to deliver a demarche of demonstration."*

His plan, the Five-Paw Proclamation, became their unwritten mandate,* their Manifesto. By Grundy's will, it was deposited in their hearts* then and there.

Five-Paw Proclamation – Grundy's master plan. Akin to a multi-point plan of the type revealed in a Presidential address to establish the major direction of intended policy.

Demarche of demonstration – The Assembly would indicate its displeasure in the only way it could – by its actions. In international politics, a demarche is usually a written communiqué between nations, formally expressing the displeasure of the sending nation in the recent actions of the other. It is a diplomatic scolding.

> **Unwritten mandate** – The Assembly's marching orders, having the force of authority. In democratic politics, an elected government perceives it has been given a mandate by the people to execute its promised actions.

> **Deposited in their hearts** – The members of the Assembly take the Five-Paw Plan as their own and agree to be bound by it. In international politics, the written instruments providing evidence of a nation's agreement to be bound – for example, to a treaty – are placed with a depositary person or organization. For example, the depositary of the Chemical Weapons Convention is the United Nations.

These were the principles of Grundy's plan:

The Five-Paw Proclamation
As justly willed by Grundy, preparatory to the proposed enactment of the

First Treaty of Tani Between The Righteous Assembly and It, The Tuleg

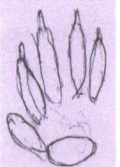 The First-Paw Mission: To Scout
Action: Hawks, Falcons, Vultures, selected songbirds, and The Girls (Girls lead)
Execution: Keep the Tuleg under constant surveillance: the birds, high; The Girls, at ground level, the Assembly to be warned of imminent provocations.

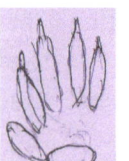 The Second-Paw Mission: To Probe
Action: Marmots and Snapping Turtle (leader: turtle Aristophelia)
Execution: Advance to within three fox-bounds of the Tuleg's den, in order to test *Its* response. This will determine whether The Tuleg will negotiate.

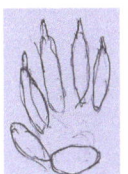

The Third-Paw Mission: To Harass
Action: Raccoons, Voles, Insects, Spiders, Rabbits, and The Girls (leader: raccoon To Be Announced – position open)
Execution: Tease, distract, annoy and frustrate The Tuleg. This will prevent *Its* mind – we assume for the present *It* has one – from placing focus on the Tani.

The Fourth-Paw Mission: To Befoul
Action: Skunks, Mice and Fox (leader: skunk Putrefacia)
Execution: Perform area denial activities. Conduct chemical missions in close proximity to the Tuleg den. Defecate at will.

The Fifth-Paw Mission: To Burrow
Action: Marmots, Rabbits, Mice, Voles and Opossums (leader: marmot Grundy)
Execution: Establish and maintain apartments in all previous camps. Double the number of apartments within three moons. Confuse and confound the Tuleg. Close proximity to the Tuleg den desired and will be rewarded, but is not required.

"The Assembly will implement these provisions in order, as willed, in a graduated response*," Grundy communicated. It became clear to all that Grundy had put considerable thought into his plan. It could actually work!

"By this method we will demonstrate our resolve," Grundy burbled, "while leaving The Tuleg some behavioral options."

"We will place ourselves in a position to negotiate, by our actions, The First Treaty of Tani, under which we will cede some of the land to The Tuleg, but only in exchange for *Its* willingness to undo some of *Its* travesties," Grundy burbled grandly.

> **Graduated response** – The Assembly would execute the missions of the Five-Paw Proclamation one at a time, intending to increase pressure on The Tuleg until *It* yielded. Sometimes used as policy in international conflict, graduated response has questionable effectiveness since it can be mistaken for weakness of the user and often serves only to progressively harden the will of its victim.

The Code of the Tani included respect for one's enemies, and the wisdom never, if eventual cooperation was desired, to close out all of the enemy's avenues of action.

Drawing upon his knowledge of this tradition, Grundy continued: "Hopefully, The Tuleg will choose the right option: to desist from *Its* destructive activities. But we will reserve the courage and the right to retaliate-in-kind* against further provocations. We will, one way or the other, show The Tuleg *It* is not welcome here!"

This last brought a rustling like wind from the observers in the trees and a great mammalian *Huzzah* from the creatures on the ground. Grundy had swayed them!

> **Reserve the right to retaliate-in-kind** – The Assembly would be willing to take whatever action is taken by The Tuleg. In politics, some treaties or agreements permit signatory states to make reservations to their provisions. For example, the single reservation of the United States to the Chemical Weapons Convention was to retain the right to retaliate-in-kind with CW against the use of CW against it or its close allies.

The Five-Paw Proclamation of the members of The Assembly was declared effectively in force* that same night. The Grand Council dissolved into high-pawing and dancing.

Effectively-in-Force – The Proclamation had the force of law, to the extent The Assembly understood law. In international politics, the text of a treaty often includes conditions which will establish its effective-in-force date, the date upon which it will become international law.

7. DEMARCHE

Ensuing events, as understood by the man: Thus began a confusing time of offense and counter-offensive, during which it was never clear who the offending party was and who were the offended, or who was attacking and who just retaliating-in-kind. It was a time when the man's actions, while deliberate and determined, were intended to discourage wildlife activity in close proximity to his house, but not necessarily to be injurious.

Ensuing events as understood by The Assembly: During this confusing time, the Assembly's actions began as defensive, but were adapted over time out of necessity to respond to The Tuleg's actions, to be both offensive and willful. For reasons of operational security,* they were contrived to look natural and harmless in both cases. This period would ultimately and forever afterward be known by The Assembly as the prelude to The Battle of The Lower Hill.

Operational Security – The Assembly does not want its true intentions to be known by The Tuleg. In politico-military affairs, operational security is comprised of the policies and methods by which the deliberate concealment of intended action or capability is accomplished.

Actions taken by the man: The man continued to unfold his plans for the property. First, he removed six acres of barley chaff and scrub brush from the property, three acres on each of the two hills, with his new riding mower. Each area was now a clean expanse that would soon become lawn. He installed a Bluebird house on a pole in front of his dwelling; a second pole behind his house supported a bird-feeder to attract the many other varieties of songbirds that were evident in the valley.

Actions taken by The Assembly: During the First Paw mission, The Assembly observed the man's continuing activities with disdain. Even the babies were indoctrinated as capable scouts, their true purpose well-concealed beneath a veil of innocence. Their reports were prompt and accurate, for example:

"He doo bad things," the burbled report of the littlest of The Girls, convinced The Assembly that The Tuleg was clearly still involved in offensive behaviors.

"We need to advance to Second Paw mission activities," burbled Priscilla 'Possum.

Three of The Girls rebutted in unison: "We rather like the new look of the land! The grass tends to grow thicker and sweeter now. Moreover, our children can now run flat out across the little knolls. Why, they were engaging in games of Let's Just Run immediately after making their first Tuleg reports!"

Grundy wondered whether he was hearing the truth from The Girls or just their spite for being cited earlier as careless in their security practices. Unsure as to whether he should believe his on-scene observers,* Grundy spit a bit of thistle-stalk and called for aerial observation.

"Well, who are you going to get to do *tha-at*?" burbled The Girls cynically.

> **Believe his on-scene observers** – Grundy questions the first-hand reports of The Assembly's scouts. In politico-military affairs, first-hand reports provide "ground truth" information, but these may be necessarily disregarded or manipulated for broader political purposes.

After he had thought about it, Grundy's first instinct was to seek confirmation of The Girls' reports by means of NTM* – Naturally Transiting Migrants. By lucky chance (good leaders are always lucky), Grundy found a gaggle of Canada Geese at rest on the upper hill only a few nights later. The geese were seasonal visitors to The Tani. The length of their tenure there could be observed in their in-flight discipline – sloppy, noisy cloud-formations while training the goslings, and sharp, quiet skeins in V-formation prior to their later migration. The advantages of enlisting the geese were that their great wings were silent, they flew low and they could put a hundred pairs of eyes on a spot within a few seconds. He hastily approached Tumugaq, their ancient leader.

> **By means of NTM** – Grundy wants a perspective other than he gets from ground-level. So do politico-military advisors, who use NTM – meaning, National Technical Means – which includes satellites and other sophisticated equipment.

Grundy knew the culture of the geese included barter. He found Tumugaq agreeable to organizing a specific training flight in exchange for the offer of The Assembly's vigilance – that is, The Assembly would stand guard in a passive way – in the flock's local nesting areas. But it wasn't easy…

"You want me to fly over a train, eh, Grandy?" burbled Tumugaq.

"No, to conduct a special training flight," responded Grundy.

Fortunately, their communication improved from there. In a few minutes, Tumugaq had assured Grundy of his support.

"Another win!" Grundy thought to himself. "If I could just get him to stop calling me Grandy!"

Tumugaq, for his part, had his own issues. The molting season had just ended, and the goslings were concurrently making their first flights under instruction. Beyond that, Tumugaq had failing eyesight. In his near-sightedness, he depended more and more on the younger geese to take the point during flights.

"And they think I am tired…ptah!" burbled Tumugaq to the wind.

More importantly, onset of dementia meant Tumugaq had bad days, during which he sometimes lost his sense of true North.

The following afternoon, it took Tumugaq several hours to organize and position the full flock. The geese were fussing with their fledglings endlessly. The fledglings just wanted to be airborne and didn't care in what direction they flew. The subsequent flight proved less than satisfactory – the sun had been allowed to get too low and distracted the young ones. The fledglings kept breaking formation to swoop when they should have been stroking, and they had to be noisily herded back. Tumugaq led because the flight was relatively short and conducted at low altitude.

His later report to Grundy was delivered in broken burbleage:

"Corn's high. Lot of corn, eh? No water, though, eh? Eastern Bluebirds everywhere, and crows. Darned things threw off my cadence. Scruffs! No Tulegs, no."

Tumugaq had put a hundred pairs of eyes on the wrong knoll! Exasperated, Grundy slapped his paws to his cheeks and called for the raptors.

The raptors circled high overhead of the lower hill for several minutes then dropped in, being so bold as to land between the Tuleg's driveway and his dwelling under the guise of conducting flight lessons. The Tuleg suspected nothing of their true purpose. The raptors' report confirmed the earlier reports given by The Girls:

"Hee! Hee bee gee bee," burbled the lead raptor, which Grundy took to mean, The Tuleg's behavior was, if anything, worsening.

The rabbits reported accurately and without further observation that they had lost whole fields of cover for morning and evening feedings and for concealment while nesting.

The existence of conflicting reports prevented consensus* on The Assembly's next steps for a time. The rabbits, outnumbering

The Girls, were eventually acknowledged by all to be enduring the greater injustice. The Five-Paw plan moved forward.

> **Prevented consensus** – The Assembly's actions are delayed by conflicting reports. In democratic political forums, decisions are most often made by consensus, meaning a majority of the members who are present and voting. Reaching consensus on difficult issues requires time and diplomacy.

8. ESCALATION

Events transpiring, according to the man: Next, he dealt with the woodchucks. His builder had left a large mound of unused topsoil near the garage. Perfect! This he used, a wheelbarrow-full at a time, to fill half a dozen chuckholes on the north side of his house. He did not wish to hurt the chucks, only to drive them into the woods. His method was to discharge insecticide spray into a hole until mist·could be seen exiting the "back door" of the hole. Then he would stand back and allow time for any hidden resident to flee the unpleasantness. When no escaping animal was evident, he assumed the burrow was empty and would use his spade to fill first one "door" and then the other. Then he would move to the next apparent dwelling and repeat the process. It seemed harmless and effective. Woodchuck sightings decreased over time.

What actually happened, according to The Assembly: Apartments had been destroyed! That was enough! Grundy invoked the Second Paw mission. Aristophelia accepted her charge, but had a dual purpose in mind. Family came first, then clan, and only then, The Assembly.* She waited several days until conditions were optimum, namely, the immediate aftermath of a booming thunder-and-lightning rainstorm that soaked the earth. Then she advanced, stealthily and all afternoon, in a treacherous climb upstream and over the rocks in the little creek from her stream-bank apartment. She emerged from the tree-line at dusk at the base of the lower hill and directly below and behind The Tuleg's dwelling. How would The Tuleg respond? As darkness fell, Aristophelia climbed the hill under brilliant starlight. At the same time, a cloudbank of fireflies provided a pyrotechnic display that both screened and enchanted her along her way.

Family came first, then clan, and only then, The Assembly – Aristophelia's value scale. In international politics and business, the value scale of family, clan, tribe, political movement or nation is encountered in middle-eastern cultures.

Aristophelia advanced to the top of the hill and within five feet of The Tuleg's dwelling. While The Assembly watched from The Tani with a hundred pairs of eyes and bated breath, The Tuleg appeared and watched Aristophelia from a distance.

Undaunted, Aristophelia ignored The Tuleg and examined bare patches of earth for suitability to her primary biological mission. After a couple of cricket songs, she found the perfect spot.

Minutes passed as Aristophelia waited in silence and apparent safety. All quiet. The Tuleg had strangely disappeared. Tree-frogs sang to her as the last shades of darkness fell. With a final glance at a reassuring moon, Aristophelia dropped to her breastplate. Then, she swept her forelegs in a breast-stroke in front of her, her claws clearing bits of grass and breaking the surface of the earth. When the soil loosened, she rose up, turned head-to-tail and began digging a hole with her hind legs. She dug until after midnight, then labored at her egg-laying mission, closing up her dig just before dawn. She assessed her work with great satisfaction, leaving a tiny hole through which a shaft of light would draw her hatchlings to The Tani and life in The Assembly.

Her retreat to the tree-line was accomplished without incident. The Second Paw mission was a complete success, as was Aristophelia's obligation to her species.

This was good news – almost too good to be true, thought Grundy. Now he wanted confirmation of the Tuleg's good intentions. Grundy took it upon himself to perform a second probing mission. The following day, Grundy approached The Tuleg's dwelling from its front by a circular route.

No apparent activity out front. From two tree-lengths away, he could see into the entrance of the dwelling – it was open, but closed at the same time by a looking-wall. What would it be like inside, he wondered? He had to know.

Grundy walked softly to the entrance, stood on hind legs and touched the looking-wall: it was hard and would not move. He sniffed at it, too, but it had no scent. There being nothing more he could do, he turned to withdraw. At the bottom of the little ledges he found a crop of yellow and purple Pansies. Grundy decided that lunch was a fair trade for no new information. The yellow ones were particularly delicious. He ate all of them.

9. RETALIATION

The truth of what happened next, according to The Assembly: During the moon that followed, The Tuleg had continued to destroy their dwellings. One by one, their apartments had been filled with earth, and worse. The Tuleg had slashed and cut down the vines along the tree-line, too, opening the deepest recesses of The Tani to a cruel sun. The Assembly's darkness, quiet and cool were diminished. Grundy himself had been attacked in the open and forced to take refuge, seeking safety but refusing to be intimidated, as his mother had taught him.

It was necessary to show more resolve.* Grundy had immediately invoked the Third Paw Mission, To Harass, and added some Rules of Embarrassment.* Then he sent them all – insects, birds, reptiles and mammals great and small – each with a different objective, to frustrate The Tuleg and thereby make a final effort to get *Its* attention.

More resolve – Grundy wants The Tuleg to understand that The Assembly is steadfast in its purpose. In international politics, it is sometimes necessary for a nation to demonstrate clear resolve in its intentions. Misinterpretation of such a signal can cause conflict, as in Saddam Hussein's misunderstanding of U.S. intentions with respect to the defense of Kuwait, resulting in the First Gulf War.

Rules of Embarrassment – Additional guidelines for Third Paw mission behavior provided by Grundy. In international conflict, democratic governments provide Rules of Engagement, or ROE, for their fighting forces. Examples of ROE include: "Do not fire unless fired upon," and "Do not engage civilian non-combatants." ROE are intended as guidelines for adherence to the Laws of War and Armed Conflict. An enemy having knowledge of specified ROE gains a distinct advantage.

For example, by day, the fox kits were to keep any birds that did not already understand the mission away from the man's bird feeder. They would be relieved of this task at dusk by young raccoons assigned to empty the feeder under cover of darkness. The Assembly's youth were particularly attracted to this Mission, many expressing their exuberance in gestures that Grundy did not fully understand.

"Can you imagine being *ordered* to eat all you can?" burbled one of the raccoons excitedly.

"But as long as they stay within my additional Rules," thought Grundy...

As the Plan went forward, First Paw-mission scouting and reporting continued...

§

Further events, according to the man:

The First Groundhog Fracas. If he didn't know better, he would have thought the animals on the property were deliberately baiting him. He had found hand-and-nose-prints on the glass of his front and back exterior doors. Some mammal – raccoon or marmot, most likely – had actually stood there and looked in! He cleaned the glass. The flowers growing in the flower pot at the front door had been destroyed, too. He replaced and repotted them.

Then one afternoon, he spotted a marmot brazenly walking across his driveway toward his front door – AHA! He had chased the intruder, which ran up the trunk of the Red Maple tree in front of his house, and out onto a limb where it sought sanctuary, not eight feet off the ground. He stood beneath the branch and scolded the critter face-to-face, in secret admiration of its grit, and it shook with fear – or perhaps, excitement - but did not move. He had moved away to allow the animal to retreat in safety, believing he had taught it a lesson it would long remember, while proclaiming to the air:

"That one won't be back, heh!"

§

The Bug Scuffle. Even the insects seemed to evince a malevolent will towards him.

"Impossible!" he murmured under his breath. As the sun warmed the days, thousands of minuscule, red Clover Mites swarmed up the walls of his house and crawled effortlessly beneath its windowsills. Then they flowed down the walls and infested the wall-to-wall carpets. The man didn't notice, but his daughter did, announcing her shrill displeasure at the invasion of her own bedroom. "Gaaa! Da-dee!"

The man had built an outdoor jungle gym for his grand-daughter. While she played there one afternoon, a large flying Assassin Bug smacked into her cheek and rebounded to her shoulder, where it sat defiant, as if asserting its aerial right-of-way. After the Bug was swept away, his grand-daughter held her hand to the side of her face and could not be consoled for several minutes.

More observant after that episode, the man found that spiders of all types could frequently be found nesting in the cracks of the pressure-treated lumber of the structure – almost as if they *preferred it* to alternate sites, he thought. One of them was a small Black Widow. He dispatched them all. Thereafter, the man carried a can of Raid insect spray whenever he approached the little playground, thinking, *come on, make my day*!

The wasps were no less offensive. In any given week, the man could find five or six Paper Wasp nests – little, upside-down umbrellas full of larvae – beneath his rain-gutters. The Mud Daubers also worked tirelessly to construct their little tunnel-nests high on the brick face of the house. The man would knock them down and have to do it again the following week. Eventually, he determined they were attracted to standing water in the open rain-gutters. He called *Thompson Creek* and had helmeted gutters installed – a $13,000 solution. Yikes!

§

The 'Coon Conundrum. The man's bird feeder, shaped like a small house with an open feeding tray in the front, held ten pounds of seed. It was supported atop a metal pole, with the pole being inserted into a metal sleeve that sunk 18 inches into the ground for stability. He had drilled a couple of holes in one side of the metal feeder and inscrted wire bag-ties in order to attach a wire mesh suet cake-holder. On the opposite side, he attached a hook from which he dangled a Finch feeder. The feeder would therefore attract many kinds of birds. The man loved to sit in his sunroom and watch birds feed there, keeping a pair of 7X35 binoculars handy for that purpose.

One day he noted a couple of young foxes, skinny as though they had just left their mother's care, playing beneath the feeder. As he watched, they dug for seeds around the base of the feeder, loosening its purchase on the lower hill. It began to tilt. After the kits had left, the man straightened the pipe and tamped the earth, then placed rocks around the base of it to discourage the kits. The kits returned the next day, and the day after that. The birds didn't. The man wondered why his seed was disappearing anyway, and in great quantity.

Then, in the dusk, he saw a raccoon hand-over-hand its way up the pole to sit on the roof of the feeder. After circling to get comfortable, the animal used its humanoid hands to scoop great handfuls of seed onto the ground. Then it used the same fingers first to taste the suet, and then to open the suet-cake holder and pull the entire cake from its container. Burdened with its loot, the 'coon then retreated down the pole, sliding as if it were a first responder in a firehouse, to the meal at hand. The man replaced the suet cake and wired the cake-holder shut with two short, twisted lengths of electric cord.

The following dusk, a raccoon – *was it the same one?* – climbed the pole, shoveled more seed to the ground and began using its fingers to again enjoy the suet cake. This time, and owing to the fact that it did not have opposable thumbs, the 'coon was unable to untwist the cord and open the cake holder.

"Ha! Gotcha!" thought the man, observing smugly from inside his house.

Then, not satisfied with a fist-full of suet, the 'coon tugged at the suet cake-holder until the bag-tie anchors let go, dropping the entire suet cake to the ground. The impact sprung open the suet cake-holder, exposing the entire cake. The 'coon then picked up both and made off with them into the woods before the man could respond.

The man purchased a new suet cake-holder. He used the existing holes in the side of the feeder to bolt-and-nut a wooden mounting plate to the side of it. He attached the new suet cake-holder to the mounting plate with a metal bracket and wood screws. Again, he placed a new suet cake inside and secured its door with twisted lengths of cord. He also purchased a large funnel that he attached to the pole, pointy end up, like the rat-guards on a ship's mooring lines, to prevent the 'coon from climbing the pole.

On the third consecutive evening, the man, feeling proud of himself, settled in early to watch a frustrated 'coon. At dusk, not one but two 'coons appeared, and the man watched slack-jawed as they used the large funnel as a step-ladder, both climbing effortlessly over it to the top of the feeder. The two jostled back and forth for purchase on the limited space while they shoveled seed to the ground, causing the feeder to wobble back and forth. The Law of Gravity soon took over as their combined weight – perhaps thirty-five pounds – toppled the entire feeder to the ground.

The suet cake-holder held, but the top of the feeder sprung open, spilling ten pounds of seed. The man interrupted their ensuing wild party using words that, he realized later, they probably didn't understand. They fled. Then he dug a one-foot-square hole a foot deep, placed the feeder's mounting sleeve upright in the center of it and poured ninety pounds of cement into the remaining hole. He reinserted the pole and bird feeder into the sleeve. Finally, he moved the funnel up higher on the pole so the 'coons would have no purchase on the pole above it.

The man derived no pleasure from frustrating 'coons with this latest modification, because the 'coons did not return to test it – *almost as if they had been militarily withdrawn*, he thought. He laughed to himself for this impossible thought.

"Naw," he said aloud, dismissing the idea.

Even so, he thought he had won.

The birds did not return to the feeder for more than a week.

10. CHEMICAL WARFARE

Further true events, as related by The Assembly: All of their previous signals had been ignored – that was the only conclusion The Assembly could draw. Moreover, the soil of the upper hill unexplainably developed the foul smell of the Tulegs, when no Tulegs had been seen there! And, some of The Assembly reported other foul smells that had made them sick during their scouting missions near the Tuleg den, even in or near their own apartments. The offensive odors were persistent and pervasive enough to obliterate the more subtle olfactory clues to other dangers in their environment. The sense of smell was so important to The Assembly's way of life that to have it compromised was untenable. Surgical use of Special Methods was required. Grundy exercised the right of The Assembly to retaliate-in-kind, and invoked the Fourth Paw mission – To Befoul.

Insects and spiders were invited to practice home-making, and thereby infest every crevice in the Tuleg den with mud, paper, grass and cobwebs. Grundy made it clear that taking up residence was optional, and discretion advised.

The birds, especially the crows, were invited to eat heavily in the evenings and to concentrate their morning constitutional flights over the airspace of The Littlest Tuleg's jungle-fort.

The male foxes were invited to mark their territory as if the Tuleg den and its den-path did not exist. This they did with wavering reliability, pursuing their own agendas instead, as Grundy had feared. When he wasn't pleading with them to let the rabbits alone, Grundy was discouraging the foxes' mating rituals – like leaving fresh-picked corncobs in plain view for the vixens to find – in favor of the anti-Tuleg Fourth-Paw mission.

The rabbits were invited to grace The Tuleg's gardens with rabbit do-do. This they did. The foxes understood their own mission, but not that of the rabbits, which seemed trivial to them. The foxes instinctively pursued the rabbits' bobbing white tails. Thus, the two coalition partners worked at cross-purposes* for a time, with the foxes diminishing the do-do damage that the rabbits might otherwise have done.

> **Coalition partners worked at cross-purposes** – The members of The Assembly sometimes unintentionally undid the work of their partners in their zeal to accomplish their own assigned missions. This is an unfortunate consequence of uncoordinated politico-military missions, even when conducted by a single country. It can be seen, for example, in past concurrent attempts to remove loose nuclear materials from and to secure loose nuclear materials within third-world nations.

The Girls were dispersed to the lawn for herd-level gastronomic activities. These missions were successfully accomplished, with The Girls then dematerializing into the underbrush, often without even being noticed by The Tuleg. The overall impact, however, was minimal owing to the unfortunate fertilizing effect of their work on the earth near the Tuleg's dwelling.

All of these Fourth Paw measures were planned by Grundy but overseen by the skunk Putrefacia to give Grundy believable blamelessness.* After being marooned on a tree limb, Grundy was not anxious for another face-to-face encounter with The Tuleg in the open field. While she proved an able field-commander, usually unhurried when under stress, Putrefacia had almost blown her own first Fourth Paw mission. She had sortied effectively enough, and without compromise, to the rear wall of the Tuleg-den. There, she held her breath and waited. Good. Nothing else moved in the darkness. Then, as she walked the wall's stony length, nose to the ground, she reached the flat place near the rear entry.

> **Believable blamelessness** – The Fourth-Paw mission is implemented in a way to protect its execution from providing evidence of or actually revealing its chief planner, Grundy. Some politico-military affairs require a head-of-state or a particular leader to have *plausible deniability* in order to be able to retain their negotiating leverage and credibility or to act as an ultimate arbiter if necessary.

When she raised her head, she beheld her own reflection a few inches away in one of The Tuleg's looking-walls! Startled, she saw in her mind's eye the usurpation of her territory by another skunk, and instinct was quicker than thought. Barrooom! She loosed her entire payload! Unfortunately, she had not fully engaged her hindquarters before discharge, the wind did not favor her, and she stood momentarily in her own cloud. Only the groans of The Tuleg from within its open apartment looking-wall above heralded a successful chemical laydown. She had been lucky-on-target.

The Assembly avoided close proximity to her for a week, and it became apparent to all that chemical dispersal by skunk could backfire. But thereafter, Putrefacia faithfully repeated her chemical mission weekly and without further incident, which was necessary in order to sustain its potency.

Unexpected random visits from neighboring dogs both assisted and thwarted The Assembly in this effort. Word had gotten out. The dogs, including a number of them venturing in from outside The Tani, scoured the lower hill around The Tuleg's den and scratched, dug, urinated and defecated profusely, it seemed, just for the sport of it. Dogs! An unwelcome and direct threat to Grundy's desire for graduated response. The dogs' clumsy approach could not be called surgical at all! The Assembly did not like or trust them, and they could not be made to follow Grundy's plan. In fact, The Assembly could not control any aspect of their behavior.

The dogs were rebels.* While they contributed somewhat to the Fourth Paw mission objectives, the downside meant The Tuleg would associate the worst of the dogs' behavior with that of The Assembly. This could thwart the conduct of diplomacy and undercut the willingness of The Tuleg toward provision of any restitution. Having entered the fray, the dogs were a threat to the very harmony The Assembly wished to restore! The dogs could not be made to see that the greater good was in unity of action. To the dogs – as with some other members of The Assembly, as Grundy would find out – their mission came first. They had not been present for the delivery of The Five-Paw Proclamation, and their unsanctioned objective could best be described as, "Have Fun! Don't Worry! Be Happy!"

> **The dogs were rebels** – The stray dogs were not under the control of The Assembly or The Tuleg, neither of which particularly liked having the dogs around. If the dogs supported The Assembly's mission, it was strictly by accident. Third parties entering international conflict – often called "rebels" – usually have their own agendas and can have the same effect as the dogs did in The Tani.

The only way for The Assembly to deal with these rebels – their own allies – was to shun them and hope they would disperse of their own volition. But the opportunity cost* of shunning was lack of situational awareness* concerning the dogs' activities. Grundy was greatly frustrated by this: a leader must have ground-truth information to be effective!

> **Opportunity cost** – If The Assembly chose not to communicate with the dogs, it would have no knowledge of what the dogs were doing until after the fact. The opportunity costs of choosing a particular politico-military policy must be considered and weighed prior to implementing the policy.

> **Situational awareness** – In order to be an effective leader, Grundy must have as much knowledge as possible about what is going on everywhere in The Tani. In international politics, providing situational awareness for leadership is the driving force behind most intelligence gathering.

Events of the same period, according to the man:

The Bug Fight. The man signed a contract with a local exterminator to spray the foundations of the house six times per year. Between the contractor's visits, the man made regular checks of the soffit and fascia beneath the overhang of his roof. He carried *Raid* or *Black Flag* spray cans each time he ventured out. This was war. Wasps, bugs and spiders were effectively eliminated from the perimeter of his home. *Take that*, you bugs!

He also installed a three-foot-wide strip of three-inch River Rock around the foundation of his home – a tiny, waterless moat that prevented direct contact of lawn and exterior wall. The strip was intended to dissuade insects from further encroachment, but this it could not do. In fact, constructing this barrier had been a futile effort.* But it looked good. And it only cost a few hundred dollars.

> **This barrier had been a futile effort** – The border of river rock around The Tuleg's dwelling would not prevent insects from reaching the house. In international politics, centuries of experience have proven fences, walls and other defensive obstructions to be ultimately ineffective in stopping the movement of people, arms and/or equipment. Examples include the East German Berlin Wall and the French Maginot Line.

The Bird Fight. The jungle-fort behind the man's house had a tent-shaped, blue-and-yellow-striped tarpaulin for a top. His grand-daughter loved the colors – but apparently, so did the birds. Shortly after he installed the top, the man noticed that the fowl activity was becoming indeed foul on that side of the house! After only a few days, the tarpaulin was blue, yellow and white! Some of the birds' calling cards had even been left on the platform beneath the tarp! How did they *do* that? Thereafter, the jungle-fort needed to be wiped down before his grand-daughter could play on it. Eventually, he bought a new tarp for a few hundred more dollars.

The Fox Fight. The foxes proved almost uncanny. For a time, a fox (at least, the man thought it was one fox) left his scat exclusively on the man's driveway. Not *near* the driveway, but exactly *on* it, as if it were a fox's territorial boundary. But the man's driveway didn't bound anything in its sinuous path to the road. Yet, he found scat decorously deposited at multiple points along its length. This development, both confusing and annoying, perturbed him. And then, periodically, the man found pieces of rabbit carcass left in the same spots. Yech! And, the fox sometimes left a corn cob or two, with the stalks peeled back, as if they were discarded garbage. Of course, the man held his breath, retrieved and then trashed all of these things.

Deer and Rabbits. The man had no quarrel with the deer or rabbits because his daughter loved them. He had planted no crops for them to destroy. He noted that the deer, while plentiful, were timid and could be trained by shooing to avoid his best plantings. Finally, the neighborhood foxes seemed to keep the rabbits' numbers in check.

The Skunk Fight. The man found the evening air clean and fresh at Quiet Light Cove, much easier to breathe than at his previous residence, he noted. *Food for the lungs*, he thought. He loved to sleep with his bedroom window open above the door to the back patio – he always slept better when he could smell the seasons. That ended one June. While he slept, a skunk unloaded directly beneath his open window. He awoke to a bedroom engulfed in the terrible odor. He shut the window immediately, but it took an hour for the exhaust fan to clear the remaining, invisible cloud from the room.

This particular evening atrocity repeated with some regularity during the summer, always while he was sleeping, and it would always awaken him. Unfortunately, the skunk's egress was swift enough that he wouldn't have had time to point a gun, even if he had a gun. In fact, he never saw the perpetrator, an outcome all the more infuriating if one wanted clues for retaliation. Fortunately, the effect lasted only a few days each time, during which the man prayed for rain to diminish the odor, slept without fresh air and ground his teeth.

The Dog Fight. The neighbor's dogs were completely unpredictable. They appeared out of nowhere, moved fast and in pairs, looked threatening and squatted everywhere. He could never be assured of their friendliness and did not trust them with his grand-daughter's outdoor safety. When they came streaking across the property, he would retreat inside.

The man did not like being denied the use of the out-of-doors in this way, but on this land, his neighbor was 200 yards distant and not a social acquaintance. In the county countryside, people tended to be independent and self-sufficient. Where police response-times were long, property security was often provided by Smith & Wesson: one did not just walk across a neighbor's ten-acre property and knock on their door unannounced, especially with a grievance. And, the man had to balance the effect of neighborhood unrest, if he were to involve the police, against his own periodic inconvenience. He decided to live and let live where his neighbor's dogs were concerned.

The stray dogs were another matter. These he reported to the county and to the police a number of times. All of his reports were futile. The man festered in his frustration.

§

But chemical warfare, it turned out, had limited tactical utility for both parties in terms of accomplishing their respective missions. Chemical activities required a lot of coordination, depended upon weather for effectiveness and infuriated the opponent beyond any inclination towards diplomacy. Or even, civility.

11. SIEGE - OPEN WARFARE

The Western Front, Battle of the Lower Hill

The Assembly's after-action report: Although few in The Assembly understood the concept, they were now locked in a battle of wills with *It*, The Tuleg. Those who had some sense of what it meant to prevail, like Grundy, refused to acknowledge any motive other than execution of their plan and restoration of order. But some in The Assembly were, by this time, invested just to win. Additionally, they thought they were beginning to sense a reluctance to continue, and maybe even a weakness, in their leader, Grundy. The opossums and foxes, who had perhaps the strongest sense of territorial imperative, were especially defiant and vowed not to yield ground.

Priscilla 'Possum, the smallest and most vocal of the group and a frequent spokes-creature for her kind in difficult times, stepped forward.

"Look," Priscilla pointed out correctly, "we have invested blood and treasure, but we mammals are not the only ones who have been hurt. The insect population has already suffered terrible losses! And you have told us we will retaliate in kind!"

Grundy sensed his control of the situation was slipping away. Things were not unfolding as he had intended. The long-term stability of The Tani was at stake.

"I can almost feel my whiskers getting gray," he burbled later to his reflection in the little stream.

For the first time in his life, he felt lonely under the burden of leadership,* a fact he found difficult to admit to himself. Then it came to him that because he *was* the leader, it fell to him to address and change the situation, and nothing would change unless and until he did so. He summoned the Central Incisors* – his closest and most trusted woodland colleagues – for a twilight meeting beneath The Protector.

> **Lonely under the burden of leadership** – Grundy recognizes his dilemma, and feels isolated by the weight of the decisions to be made. The Assembly looks to him for answers that none of the rest of them can give. In politico-military affairs, this concept is referred to as *the loneliness of command.*

> **Central Incisors** – Grundy consults his most trusted advisors to assist in decision-making. In politics, many heads-of-state have similar advising bodies; for example, a President's Cabinet or a U.S. Policy Coordinating Committee.

Those present included two of his own kind, Putrefacia - by now a seasoned mission commander, and a fox. A second invited fox was absent without leave. Finally, the group included Priscilla 'Possum. Grundy knew he needed to sway her to his support.*

> **Sway her to his support** - Grundy knows Priscilla is highly influential within The Assembly. Within each government organization, and even in subsets of government and the military, are influential persons who exercise an informal leadership. For example, Henry Kissinger was the virtual architect of U.S. foreign policy while serving as National Security Advisor during the Nixon administration.

True to form, Priscilla spoke first, her agitation evident in the thrash of her prehensile tail as she addressed The Incisors. But she looked directly at Grundy:

"I agree with those of The Assembly who mourn our collective losses and abhor change. But we must prevail!" The down-Doppler in the tone of her growling revealed she had thought about this and was not pleased, was in fact upset, and perhaps even afraid.

The others chimed in: "Yes, yes! What about all the apartments we have lost? We're not the ones causing all this trouble!"

Grundy, surprised at the depth of their apprehension, drew a breath. Stakes were high – he could lose their support and his leadership along with it. What would happen to The Tani then?* He sensed he had no choice but to implement the Fifth Paw mission - To Burrow. This he did, in spite of the feeling in the pit of his stomach, like the fluttery tickle he got when sliding down the slippery slant* into his apartment. But this time, it was tinged with nausea, and it was not a good feeling.

> **What would happen to The Tani then?** It is not uncommon for a strong leader to anticipate or attribute the failure of the (his) state to be a consequence of his removal from power.

> **Slippery slant** – Grundy implements the Fifth Paw mission in spite of feeling compelled to do so against his better judgment. He is unsure that this is the right thing to do. In politico-military affairs, this conundrum – in which certain negative outcomes occur almost unavoidably of their own accord once a particular first step is taken – is known as a *slippery slope*.

There were a number of volunteers for the first Fifth Paw assignment. Many in The Assembly were burrowers. The Incisors favored sending the marmot Susie, and after brief discussion, selected her. They knew her beauty would appeal to *It*, and thereby keep her from harm while she worked.

Approaching the Tuleg's apartment undetected proved easy for Susie. She burrowed beneath the steep wooden den-path behind the dwelling, a cool, dry place with few streaks of sunlight. Several days passed without incident. Feeling more confident and curious as well, Susie ventured out. She found a comfortable spot, and, disregarding Grundy's advice against expanding the mission*, basked in the sun on top of the wooden

den-path only a twig's distance from The Tuleg's looking-wall! Two more uneventful days passed. Susie congratulated herself and reveled in her defiance of The Tuleg. She began basking for longer periods and with her back to the Tuleg den because this afforded the best view of The Tani. During her sun-bathing, she sometimes groomed her teeth by chewing away the inviting sharp edges on the entrance to the Tuleg den...

Expanding the mission – Susie attempts to do more than Grundy has asked of her. Her actions are beyond her guidelines. Sometimes, in international affairs, circumstances dictate the use of applied resources – people and materiel – for purposes beyond those originally intended. Often, this is called *mission-creep*.

§

The man's after-action report: The man had built a small wooden porch on the rear of the house, with a few stairs leading to the lawn. One day he found what looked like a chuck-hole just underneath the platform. He filled it and packed the dirt hard. Within three days he found it open again. Again he refilled it, and placed a scrap piece of medium-density fiberboard over the hole. Two days after that, the board had been chewed and moved, and the hole had been reopened. He repeated his procedure a third time, again placing the medium-density fiberboard over the hole, but this time dropping two heavy jack-stands – used for raising his car for repair work – on top of the MDF to hold it in place. He chuckled to himself at his superiority of resources and intelligence.

Two days later, the man found a mound of dirt on top of the medium-density fiberboard, and upon further inspection, found a new hole – not under the platform, but under the bottom step – where the MDF could not be placed and where he could not reach it. His anger flared.

The man contemplated his next move for a few days that week. Then one afternoon, he saw a woodchuck sitting on his porch in the sun with its back turned toward the house! This act made the game personal – her overt presence repudiated his sovereignty*, and her posture inferred deliberate insult into the bargain! He rushed to the back door, where he stopped short with his hand on the doorknob as he looked through the glass. The animal was petite, beautiful and obviously female. She was dark, for a marmot, with sharp features that made her look like, well, a seal. He saw her vulnerability, too, and could not bring himself to harm her. Biting his lip, he merely startled her and shooed her away. But he was frustrated by her casual presence and knew she would return.

> **Repudiated his sovereignty** – In international politics, an enemy's presence near another's national border is often perceived as a threat to the other's sovereignty.

That was before he noticed the damage to his exterior door moldings, when his anger flared again! He grabbed a crowbar and ripped the porch off the back of the house (the treated lumber was a few years old and beginning to deteriorate anyway, he rationalized to himself). Then he dug up the jack-stands and the MDF and filled the new hole under the step.

Not two days after that, the man was out weeding the lawn. He rounded the back corner of the house and saw the hind-quarters of the same chuck sticking out of the new hole while she groomed its re-opened entrance! He yelled at her – GET **OUT**! – intending to chase her away, but she went *in*, instead! Whereupon, he man-handled a 90-pound sack of dry cement from the garage to the hole, mixed half of it in a bucket, and poured the slurry into the hole.

§

The Assembly's after-action report, further comment: Almost a moon passed without a report from Susie. The Assembly, alarmed and apprehensive, accepted The Incisors' urgent recommendation to send Priscilla to find or rescue her. Priscilla followed Susie's scent, and easily found her apartment site close to the Tuleg den. But having tunneled in, Priscilla found the apartment empty, and its rooms not big enough for her own girth. Out of instinct, she dug further for safety, enlarging and going beyond Susie's rooms to beneath the hard gray cliff she found there. Priscilla dug and dug. In the process, *oh horror*, she scratched up a jaw bone and some vertebrae!

The same night, she reported "The innocent have been killed!"

Of course, The Assembly could never be sure, but…none of them ever saw Susie again.

§

The Southern Front, Battle of the Lower Hill

The man's report on this theater: After (ahem) cementing the situation on the west side of his house, the man became more diligent about checking his home's foundation. In one such sweep, he noted a hole close to the basement wall on the south side. It was on the south wall that the peak of the hill, at the front of the house, swept downhill to the rear patio, which had allowed his contractor to install an English basement with windows at the home's back corner. This hole had appeared concurrent with the man's discovery of scat on the driveway in front of the house, causing him to deduce the hole most likely belonged to a fox.

The hole had been located near the peak. But wait! He discovered a smaller hole near the English basement windows, perhaps a second entrance to the same fox-hole. When he probed it gently, the earth began to fall away, proving its function as a concealed second entrance. Aha! This was all the incentive the man needed to fill the upper hole and to spray insecticide directly into the downhill hole, after which he covered it as well and waited. But there was no apparent movement or attempt at escape.

§

The Assembly's report on the southern front: While the man battled with woodchucks on the west side of his house, an observing fox determined that the marmots should not have an exclusive right to the Tuleg's hill. In fact, the fox had always wanted an apartment on that hill. Observing more closely now, he approved the south side of the dwelling as a fit place for an apartment. The fox undertook an independent mission, and after a couple of hours of digging, had established himself there. Grundy had been correct in predicting that the fox could not be trusted and would not adhere to the established Rules of Embarrassment or to Grundy's directives.

But the errant fox never returned to The Assembly. With Susie and the fox now both missing, The Assembly deduced that in war, the same plan, however well-executed, never works twice.

§

The Northern Front, Battle of the Lower Hill

The Assembly's report: The Girls ate the red bushes on the far side of the Tuleg dwelling. All of them. In fact, they dug and chewed until they destroyed everything else The Tuleg had planted there, too. Their resident buck reveled in grooming his antlers in the forsythia, snapping its branches and pruning sections of it ankle-high.

Next to engage were the voles who burrowed tunnels across the grassy areas of the lower hill. They especially enjoyed burrowing under the large cover that The Tuleg had placed on the ground around the jungle-fort where grass did not grow. The decaying grass beneath the cover had a sour, tangy taste, and the cover provided a measure of protection from the untrustworthy foxes. Soon, the voles had multiplied so rapidly that even the hungry renegade foxes could not stop their labor. They made a miniature no-man's land of trench-work that wrecked what little lawn The Tuleg had cultivated. And it was fun!

§

The man's report on the northern front: The man had planted Fire Bush and Burning Bush plants that were advertised as 'deer resistant'.

"Hah!" he shouted to the wind. "Someone has obviously forgotten to tell the deer!" Whenever he caught them in the attack, he would rattle their timidity by loudly shooing them away. No matter. They could not be deterred. They even dug up and ate the cat-o'-nine-tail bulbs he had planted in a low swale to catch runoff. After a time, with the plants thoroughly damaged, he stopped any pretense of landscaping.

And the voles! Their tunneling made the entire north yard squishy to walk on! They even went under the blue tarp – all 2100 square feet of it – that he had placed beneath and around his grand-daughter's jungle-gym. Then, the foxes ripped the tarp to get at the voles! He cut the shredded tarp away, discarded it, and allowed the grass to grow wild.

§

Meanwhile, Back at the Western Front...

The Assembly reported: Priscilla continued her Fifth Paw mission engagement in the apartment originally built by Susie.

"There has to be some practical gain from harassing The Tuleg," she thought to herself. "Otherwise, I'm just wasting my energy."

Priscilla found it easy to be comfortable in this apartment. The opening afforded easy access and the inspirational view put three full curls in her tail each time she indulged it. She would be a permanent resident here, she had decided. So, she exercised her natural remodeling skills, adding rooms for each of her children and doubling the size of her own. She also expanded the passageways, noting as she dug that while the main path allowed her to dig down, one passage had a big flat rock that prevented her from digging up. She avoided that one.

Priscilla could tell that The Tuleg still wanted the apartment because of *Its* interest in the opening and the foul smells of things that *It* left there. Her routine housekeeping took care of those while giving evidence of her mission success – The Tuleg must surely be frustrated. "*Having* is better than *wanting*," she burbled to herself in a gloat.

Then came the days of the new nasty smell. Some wood-mate had laid smelly eggs in her apartment while she slept, it seemed, but she had never seen their kind – white and round. They were too repulsive to be eaten and, although she had considered it anyway, would not have been substantial enough for a meal. She didn't want to touch them. After two days of living with the offensive odor and based upon her success to date, Priscilla self-declared her Fifth-Paw mission complete. She made a mental note of the apartment's attractiveness for future use and walked quietly away.

LOCATION, LOCATION, LOCATION!

And the man reported: The hole near the back of his house had opened up again.

"What on earth is in there now?" he asked the air in exasperation.

He poured vinegar into the hole with zero effect on its occupancy. He tried ammonia – no effect. He dropped a pressurized can of roach-bomb insecticide as far down the hole as he could get it, where it hissed away its entire contents for five minutes. Evidence of occupancy remained the following morning. The man considered gasoline but wondered if, by using all these chemicals, he might be mixing together a homemade bomb beneath his house. He balked at the thought of a headline, *"MAN RIDS PROPERTY OF MARMOT, HOUSE."*

His colleagues at work advised, "Put used cat-litter in there. Cats are predators – other animals will evacuate."

This he could do by virtue of being – um, blessed – as First Footman to a pair of felines in his home. He promptly administered two gallon-size plastic bags of the foul stuff, but the only thing that was evacuated was the used cat-litter – which he found scattered outside the hole a day later. Then by sheer luck the man entered conversation with a pest exterminator at a party.

"Moth balls," the exterminator said. "They are harmless to mammals, but critters don't like the smell. Or you could buy a gun."

So the man bought mothballs instead of a gun and dumped half of the box into the hole. He didn't see the occupant leave, but found apparent opossum tracks in the mud two days later. The tracks began at the hole and led away from his house. The apparent win was worth the persistent smell, and yes, even the nausea he would feel over the next two weeks whenever he worked in the yard behind the house.

§

At this point, neither The Assembly nor the man was approaching their desired solution, and neither was fully aware* of their effect upon the other.

> **Neither was fully aware.** This is to reflect the reality that in international conflict, the arguments of opposing parties frequently abbreviate – some would say, blur – the truth over time, while failing to directly address the underlying differences between the needs of the parties.

§

And Back at The Northern Front...

The Assembly proudly but sadly reported: Ali Musmus and his kin followed The Girls and the voles, executing their Fifth Paw mission by scouting all around the Tuleg dwelling for places to enter or to burrow. Some went up into the white tunnels at the corners of the big den, while others climbed on top of it, where other, smaller cracks and holes allowed a begrudging entrance. Sometimes, they chewed their way in. They nibbled at everything, sampling their findings for flavor and utility of later use within their own dwellings.

While the clan explored elsewhere, Ali climbed the front wall of the Tuleg dwelling. Suddenly The Tuleg emerged and Ali froze, not five tail-lengths above The Tuleg's head. Ali's eyes widened as The Tuleg's head turned in his direction. The Tuleg's eyes widened, too. Ali, certain that he had been b.u.s.t.e.d. – brought under scrutiny that ends in death – scrambled upward for his life.

The Tuleg disappeared back into his dwelling, but only momentarily. Soon he reappeared carrying a shiny Tuleg-thing of unknown purpose. All of the clan members within earshot tucked their tails between their legs as the thing made a terrible noise they had never before heard. Balang! Trabang! Balang! Trabang! Then they ran. What had he done to them? Were they going to die?

When Ali reached the roof he checked himself – no apparent damage. Seconds later he dared to look back. The Tuleg had disappeared around the side of the big apartment. Ali knew this because the noise had not stopped. Whatever the terrible consequences might be, The Tuleg continued to administer the same fate to Ali's other kin at work on all sides of the dwelling.

The Musmus clan fled blindly and in panic. But not all of them could be accounted for when later they gathered in fear for mutual comfort. Ali and one of his brothers could not be found among them. Nor did they ever return.

All in The Assembly believed the two had sacrificed themselves deliberately for the good of The Tani – they were heroes, as was Susie before them. The Musmus brothers were declared M.I.A. – Mousing in Absentia. The Assembly has ever since known the lower hill as Musmus Hill, and its ground is revered by all.

Ali Musmus M.I.A.

§

And the man reported, with some smugness: The man had been picking up mouse droppings for several days from beneath the electric porch lamps on the wall outside his front door.

"Do mice sit on those fittings, six feet up the brick wall, and catch insects at night?" he wondered. "Are they hiding behind the same brass fittings right now? How can they fit back there?" The mouse droppings cooperated only reluctantly with his broom and dustpan each time he cleared them away.

Then one afternoon he stepped outside for a walk. As he had been doing lately, his eyes made a visual sweep of the porch for mouse droppings, then up the wall to the left porch lamp. Nothing there. As his eyes scanned from the left lamp to the right, he locked in a beady-eyed stare with a mouse directly over his head and just out of reach.

"You little bandit!" he exclaimed. His fingers involuntary flexed, wanting a neck to choke. He ducked back into the house seeking a weapon. From his kitchen cupboard the man selected the lid of a five-gallon cookpot.

"Now something heavy," he said to himself. "Ah, the meat tenderizer will do."

Wielding the two, he emerged armed as a gladiator at the front of the house, where he witnessed the mouse making a clean getaway above his head. The mouse disappeared onto the roof. The man used words for which The Assembly had no translation. After a moment of thinking that he had been foiled came awareness that he brandished the world's largest mouse-gong in his hands. He filled the air with his angst: Barang! Barang! He really let them have it!

Wanting to frustrate the mouse as much as possible and to discourage other mice, he ran around the outside of the house ringing the gong continuously.

"You are not going to have an avenue of escape," he shouted to the invisible mouse. The man winded himself after two full circles but, for good measure, played an additional 30-second tattoo at the mouse's front door hangout.

"And don't come back!" he shouted in conclusion. A bandage fit neatly across the knuckle he had struck with the meat tenderizer while running. He put his grandfather's bench-mounted machine vice to good use in straightening the handle of the large lid. The dents in its circumference were another matter. In consolation, he afterward saw no more droppings at the front door. Nor did he see any more mice, anywhere around his house.

"This puts a '1' in the 'win' column," he allowed himself to think. "But where are they?"

Well, they were there. He just didn't see them.

12. CEASE FIRE

Life according to Grundy: Long days of vigilant stalemate followed Grundy's easing of Fifth Paw mission sorties. Priscilla and the Musmus clan had clearly achieved their difficult objectives and retreated. Grundy had withdrawn the rest of The Assembly, which resorted to a modified First Paw mission, woodland analysts conducting BDA – Burrowing Damage Assessment.

"Now what?" was the big burble forming in all their heads…

Grundy blinked awake. Morning shadows crept away as sunlight climbed down the trees toward the floor of The Tani. Grundy watched the garbage truck – although he did not know that was its function – as it rocked along the gravel road and submerged beyond the last knoll, out of his sight. The sounds of Tuleg-porters had become a feature of the environment and no longer bothered The Assembly as much as they once had. The road remained quiet for the remainder of the morning. In fact, The Tani including Musmus Hill would be quiet for most of the day.

The Assembly soon began to resume habitual behaviors curtailed under Five-Paw discipline. The Girls avoided dining near the Tuleg den but restarted their twilight tours across its grassy expanses. There, they gamboled or grazed unmolested. The raccoons revisited the Tuleg's relocated bird feeder, satisfied now to forage beneath it, equally unmolested. Priscilla trotted openly along the wood-line behind the Tuleg dwelling, the quickest route from one end of The Tani to the other.

"I must find a good limb, and I have little time," she burbled to herself.

Her haste spoke of her concern, not for the Tuleg but for the four honeybee-sized babies in her pouch. Turkeys still stayed to the woods, clucking the cadence of their slow-march along the banks of the little creek. But their sentinel eyes focused on the path ahead, not the Tuleg den. Even the squirrels had stopped waiting for the other nut to drop. Eventually, the frequency of

The Assembly's reports to Grundy tapered off, finally ending in disinterest. Again Grundy called The Central Incisors together:

"The Tuleg has ceased inventing new ways to disrupt our peace and quiet," he burbled.

"When I thee him," whispered a fox with a missing tooth, "Heeth motht often clothe to hith apartment. Usually, heeth feeding thumthing to the land or the birdths."

"And the grasses are greener than before," offered another groundhog. Grundy concurred in his cousin's assessment.

"I think the bad smells on the upper hill and around the Tuleg den are going away," burbled Priscilla, "or am I spending too much time with Putrefacia?"

All agreed the relative serenity of recent days confirmed that a semblance of order had been restored to The Tani.

Finally, it dawned on them that in a manner of speaking The Assembly had won. They were jubilant! Eyes wide, they jumped in the air and burbled unintelligibly. The fox ran off to mark territory with scat. In behaviors uncharacteristic of their glee, the remainder reached as high as they could on the trunks of the nearest trees and carved their victory marks, or scratched them into the soil. That night, they turned glowing eyes thankfully skyward and listened. Grundy dissolved the coalition he had formed under The Five-Paw Proclamation in a celebration of bitter-sweet triumph.

The Assembly's final assessment included that some had gone M.I.A. to retain what had always been their own. Most of them acknowledged this fact as the terrible but necessary price of confrontation. And The Tani in which they would live would be different, but would still be The Tani they loved. The members of The Assembly would resume their independent lives, but now with a collective knowledge and some understanding of The Tuleg and *Its* ways.

§

The Man's Reflections: Following his successful mouse-gonging, the man took note that wildlife activity had diminished. It wasn't that the wildlife had disappeared, just that things seemed to have settled down. After a few days' time the birds returned to his newly-relocated feeder. So did the raccoons, who surprised him by no longer attempting to climb it. Deer grazed his lawn but remained at a distance from the house. In fact all of the woodland mammals seemed to be staying closer to the woods and away from his hill.

It dawned on him that in a manner of speaking he had won! He poured a shot of celebratory Kahlua into his coffee. He laughed to himself as he raised his mug, while his eyebrows scrunched together reflectively.

"What exactly did I do to make it so?" he asked himself.

In subsequent weeks the man's focus returned to working the land that he loved. He purchased an aerator to pull behind his riding mower, spending an afternoon in the shade of a straw hat as the machine churned away behind him. He seeded the grass. He planted a column of cherry trees along the driveway and a phalanx of Scotch pine on the upper hill. "We're just farmers at heart," he confessed to the garden beds as he weeded and mulched. Each day he stepped from his doorway refreshed and returned at twilight, exhausted and content.

The siren call of the land could be particularly strong. One afternoon as he labored to plant a maple tree the man froze, swept unexpectedly by a feeling that this was where he was meant to be - that all was right with the earth and nothing else mattered - that he had been blessed beyond measure with this little piece of earth. His spade dropped with a 'klunk'. Overwhelmed, he fell to his knees in a sob and plunged his hands into the earth. He raised his head to the sky, thanked God for feeling alive in this way. Then the revelation came, of what it meant to the creatures of The Tani to dig in this same earth, their home. And he repeated the message aloud: "They live here, I'm just occupying."

"I wish I could speak to them," thought the man. He didn't know it yet, but it was his first burble...

§

So, Grundy's implementation of the Five-Paw Proclamation had affected some change in The Tuleg's behavior, after all. The First Treaty of Tani never opened for negotiation and yet Grundy was affirmed in his leadership. The Assembly survived, flourished and continued to hold The Tani beloved in its collective heart. The Tuleg, for his part, looked upon The Assembly in a new way.

The honest among them would remember that, in spite of the fact that both sides had given some credence to the other's interests, neither The Tuleg nor The Assembly could move unassisted beyond the limits of their paradigms for coexistence.* Movement required inspiration…or intervention. Some, like the opossums, would always find it difficult to grasp that compromise, not war, would keep their world on its axis.

Paradigms for coexistence - The Tuleg and The Assembly never see completely eye-to-eye. In international affairs, some differences between peoples have historically proven irreconcilable. But not ALL differences. Thus the basis for the diplomacy of negotiation.

---

13. ARMISTICE

From where he nestled in the warmth of Musmus Hill, Grundy stood erect in the middle of a chew. Dancing across the valley, a light breeze had slipped off the upper hill and passed through his whiskers, sweet and fresh with the green scents of new grass and succulent dandelion. Grundy inhaled deeply and drooled.

"Ah, greening time!" he burbled to himself.

Then he alerted. Six tree-lengths beyond and above the upper hill of The Tani, his eyes caught the movement of *another* Tuleg on the adjacent knoll. The New Tuleg was at work outside what appeared to be *another* Tuleg den.

He sighed. Although the New Tuleg actually stood outside The Tani, it would be prudent to establish a forward presence* of The Assembly to provide early warning of any future encroachment. Hopefully it would not be necessary for The Assembly to teach *It*, the New Tuleg, about ownership as it had done for The Tuleg of The Tani. He knew how to do that now. But after his success of the previous season, his natural tendency toward diplomacy had only strengthened. Quicker action on his part now might save a few apartments.

"The situation may even require another Grand Council," he burbled. Consensus on any new mission would be difficult to achieve in the five-paw-weary Assembly, but as a good leader, he trusted himself and his instincts. He began to formulate a contingency Proclamation in his mind. "Perhaps some theoretical fence-lines* for behavior, just in case," he burbled to himself. At that point his empty stomach growled, pulling his thoughts away. He began to forage.

Forward presence – Grundy wants to keep the threat of the New Tuleg away from The Tani. Politico-military activity is often based on providing similar forward presence as a buffer for national security. The axiom is *better to fight them there than here.*

Theoretical fence-lines – Grundy wants to suggest, or to impose, reasonable limits on the New Tuleg's activities before they become fact. This is also a current political tool, sometimes known as *red-lines.*

---

§

The man sat in a lawn chair on his new deck, now built larger and closer to the tree-line. He watched the trees toss gently, reminded of sea current moving grasses on reef-rock. He had turned his collar up against the breeze. His hands held a mug of coffee, the warmth of the brew easing stiffness there and warming his throat. He sipped the air as a chaser. He had not seen groundhogs for several weeks. They had been building, too, making new dwellings but now farther from his house. Their digging no longer bothered him – well, at least not as much as it once did. The land continued to call him to care for it and he reveled in exhausting himself with yard work. Today would be no different.

§

While the man mused Grundy appeared, seemingly undaunted by the man's presence. He stepped from the woods' edge and began his morning patrol for just the right cuisine. He looked up at a blue sky dome, cloudless except for a few white horsetails sweeping the stratosphere. Sunlight streaked through the trees. The Tani bathed beneath it, beautiful and quiet. His ears detected only Protector, making that sacred sound again. He exhaled slowly, the air whistling softly past his lower incisors.

"It would be a good day to dig," he thought to himself.

His limp identified him to the man as Grundy foraged back and forth, a little sailboat tacking toward the new deck on the sea of grasses. Grundy plucked a leaf of thistle. Then he alerted for the second time that morning, spotting movement near the big den. He stood on his hind legs – yes, it was The Tuleg of The Tani. They locked eyes.

For the first time in his life, Grundy did not run when surprised, as his mother had taught him. Grundy did not drop flat – in fact, he remained standing tall. For the first time, The Tuleg did not pursue. Instead, they eyed each other warily but with respect. An observer might have seen two boxers in their neutral zones anticipating a referee's decision.

After a long moment's pause, while still on hind feet, Grundy casually placed the thistle in his mouth and began a laconic chew. He kept his eyes locked on The Tuleg. An honest smile grew across The Tuleg's face. The man stood, too. Grundy stopped chewing. They regarded each other thoughtfully across 90 feet of lawn and the chasm of their separate lives.

Slowly the two turned away, drawn by the lure of the day within The Tani's embrace.

The End.

AFTERWORD

The Protector, crowned with a cloud, towers over a portion of
The Tani as Grundy sees it from his new apartment on Musmus
Hill

As the photographs attest, most events and occurrences
described in this story actually happened. The Tuleg remains in
residence on the lower hill. So does Grundy. For the present, a
state of wary peaceful coexistence subsists between The Tuleg
and The Assembly.

The idea that animals communicate with each other would
seem an unproven certainty. The occurrence of the Grand
Council exactly as written remains in question although evidence
of animal collaboration abounds. While Gundy's drafting,
delivery and implementation* of the Five-Paw Proclamation may
be improbable, the Tuleg can find no other set of possible
circumstances which quite explains events observed in The Tani.

> **Drafting, delivery and implementation** – In international politics, the drafting of policy and its ultimate implementation are two entirely different fields of endeavor, requiring different sets of expertise and usually conducted by different sets of people. As even Grundy discovered in dealing with the foxes, misrepresentation and even distortion of intended policy is a periodic and inevitable result.

In order to present this manuscript, it became necessary to conform* the language of The Tuleg with the languages and dialects of various woodland creatures. The author apologizes to The Assembly for any resulting inaccuracies.

The Tuleg suffers a nagging uncertainty as to whether he possesses greater intellect than The Assembly, and while painful to admit and uncomfortable to endure, sincerely hopes the uncertainty remains untested, especially by the raccoons.

Finally, the author wishes to acknowledge the contributions of a veritable Assembly of Tulegs of his own and other clans, for the inspiration to write – especially the influence of clans Daly-Lipe, Fargo, Schambach and Snyder.

To Conform – International treaties and agreements are drafted in "official" language versions as determined by their signatories. For bilateral agreements between two countries, there are typically two different language versions, and for multilateral treaties, as many as five or more official language versions. The texts of these versions must be conformed, that is, made to express the same meaning by interpreters in order to provide for uniform implementation of the agreements by the parties. For example, in conforming the texts of the *U.S. – U.S.S.R. Bilateral Verification Experiment and Data Exchange*, interpreters explained it was necessary to accommodate the fact that the Russian language had no present participle, *ing*; and the closest Russian translation of the English "hydraulic ram" was "water sheep." Accurate translation circumnavigates such differences.

And of course, the author is The Tuleg of the Tani.

www.ingramcontent.com/pod-product-compliance
Lightning Source LLC
Chambersburg PA
CBHW050807290526
45792CB00001B/18